SCHERENSCHNITTE

Designs and Techniques for
the Traditional Craft
of Papercutting

Susanne Schläpfer-Geiser

SCHERENSCHNITTE

Designs and Techniques for the Traditional Craft of Papercutting

Susanne Schläpfer-Geiser

Lark Books
Asheville, North Carolina

Illustrations: Sabina Nüssli Baltensweiler, CH-Horgen
Photography: Heinz Studer, CH-Bern
Production: Celia Naranjo
Translation from the German: Mary Killough

Library of Congress Cataloging-in-Publication Data
Schläpfer-Geiser, Susanne
      Scherenschnitte : designs and techniques for the traditional craft
of papercutting / Susanne Schläpfer-Geiser.
            p. cm
      Translated from the German.
      ISBN 1-887374-18-3
      1. Paper work.   I. Title.
TT870.S297   1997   96-38344
736' . 98—dc20   CIP

10 9 8 7 6 5 4 3 2 1

Published by Lark Books, 50 College St., Asheville, NC 28801

Originally published as Susanne Schlapfer-Geiser, *Scherenschnitte*, Verlag Paul Haupt
   (Bern, Stuttgart, Wien), 1994.

Copyright © 1994 Paul Haupt Publishers, Berne

English translation copyright © 1996 Lark Books

Distributed in the U.S. by Sterling Publishing
            387 Park Ave. South, New York, NY 10016; 800/367-9692
Distributed in Canada by Sterling Publishing,
            c/o Canadian Manda Group, One Atlantic Ave., Suite 105, Toronto,
            Ontario, Canada M6K 3E7

Every effort has been made to ensure that all the information in this book is accurate. However,
due to differing conditions, tools, and individual skills, the publisher cannot be responsible for
any injuries, losses, or other damages that may result from the use of the information in this
book.

ISBN 1-887374-18-3

CONTENTS

FOREWORD

I am pleased that the book market is being enriched with a new work on the subject of scherenschnitte. In contrast to the technical books about scherenschnitte that have appeared in recent years and that are largely biographies, the present work is interesting for both beginners and advanced students of scherenschnitte. The latter group will find the historical part of the book of special interest.

Susanne Schläpfer is foremost among Swiss scherenschnitte artists. Her unsurpassed works, mostly cut without a pattern, have enlivened the field of scherenschnitte in Switzerland for years. A self-taught artist, she has contributed to the spread of the old handicraft in numerous courses and demonstrations. Her book passes on many tricks and secrets to beginners. I would like to congratulate her heartily and wish her much success with the book.

—*Fritz Hobi*
Director, Winterthur Craft Museum
January 1994

INTRODUCTION

It is thanks to many people that I was able to create this book. I especially thank my mother, who awakened in me an interest in paper. Besides all the other work she did, she used to create figures from paper that were cut double and tied together at the top so that they could stand. She set my creativity in motion, which developed further by self-instruction and which has never been exhausted since my first experiments during my childhood. Over time scherenschnitte has continually changed, been refined, and new themes added. But one thing has not changed: I continue to be inspired by this activity. I have been able to show the results of my fascination at many exhibitions at home and abroad.

After 40 years of scherenschnitte experience, I am putting everything I know about it in this book with the hope that interested persons will find inspiration and the necessary instructions to produce it. Beginners should start with simple cutting, which can be very enjoyable. Perfection comes from practice; this book shows the way to success.

I have an additional wish for this book: that it help to bring interested persons closer to this old handicraft and help spread scherenschnitte.

I would like to thank my son David for typing my manuscript, mostly at night, on the computer.

I thank the director of the Craft Museum of Winterthur, Fritz Hobi, for allowing me to examine books on scherenschnitte, some very old, for the historical part of the book. He has greatly promoted scherenschnitte in Switzerland. His first Swiss Scherenschnitte Exhibition in 1985 brought together for the first time works of contemporary scherenschnitte artists.

I want to thank the many participants in my courses, who have become dear to me and whose questions and problems have taught me a great deal.

An important counterpart in my work is Mr. Kürsteiner of Zollikerberg, who is an excellent scissors grinder, because what would a scherenschnitte artist be without perfect scissors?

Christine Bachmann of Limbach-Oberfrohna, Germany, allowed me to use several cuttings from the large number of her scherenschnitte creations for the chapter on "Folded Cutwork." I wish to thank her for that.

—Susanne Schläpfer-Geiser
January , 1994

1. Materials & Tools

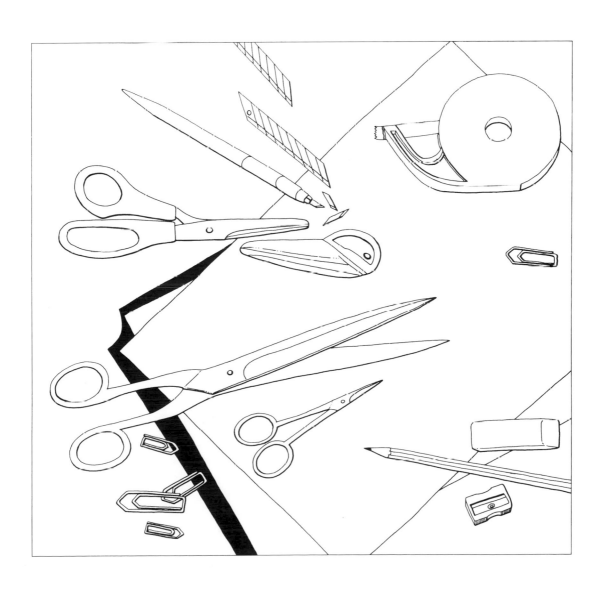

Scherenschnitte, a craft dating back hundreds of years, is still very popular. Certainly an important reason for this success lies in the fact that this handicraft requires very few tools and no elaborate setup. The materials and tools are easy to acquire, and everyone can afford them. All that's necessary are scissors, a craft knife, a pencil, and paper. A very portable craft, scherenschnitte can be carried along to help pass the time if you are kept waiting for an appointment.

Scherenschnitte makes you look at things closely. Corrections are often difficult since you cannot make a different animal from an unsuccessful horse. Therefore, it's important that you carefully examine the animals, plants, and people you want to reproduce.

The Scissors

These are the most important tool for scherenschnitte. Purchase the best scissors, even if they are the most expensive. It is important that they be made of hard steel and take a sharp edge. Scherenschnitte scissors must have narrow edges and long angles. The tips must be as sharp as knives at the top and on the sides (Fig. 1.1). Some shops sell scissors designated as scherenschnitte scissors, but they are not always suitable and may need to be resharpened. In any case, a person who sharpens knives can grind scissors of good quality so they are like those shown in the illustration. Only hard steel maintains a sharp point. If the material is weak, the tips of the

scissors will bend easily, as they are especially sensitive. Because bent tips and nicks in the cutting edges can result from dropping the scissors on the floor or even on a table, be careful to select a grip that fits your hands. If dull cutting edges and nicks are reground too often, the blades will become too short (because every time the scissors are sharpened, they become shorter). If you are handy, you can sharpen the scissors yourself with a whetstone and water, but that requires practice and a certain talent.

If you do drop the scissors and the tips are bent, it is often possible to repair the damage and restore the scissors to usefulness by drawing the tips under a piece of light cardboard, using light

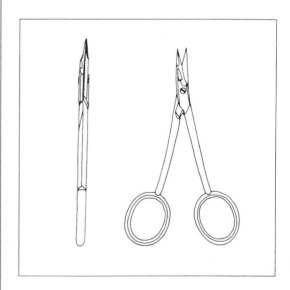

Fig. 1.1 Scherenschnitte scissors must be ground as illustrated. In contrast to other scissors, they have narrow cutting edges. With the proper scissors you can cut out a rectangular opening with sides a fraction of an inch long (1 mm) without any problem and without tearing the paper.

pressure until they are straightened out again. This method is possible only if used immediately. If you wait and let the scissors lie around too long, the tips may break off when you try to correct the problem later.

Use these scissors only for scherenschnitte. Normal paper scissors are better suited for the preparation work.

When cutting, the side of the scissors with the head of the screw showing should face the paper (Fig. 1.2). The scissors will cut better this way. If the scissors are held in the opposite direction, often the paper will not be cut but only bent downward.

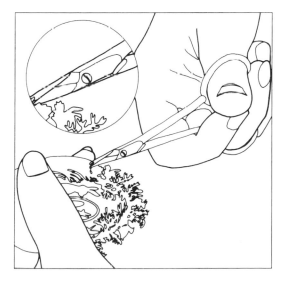

Fig. 1.2 Hold the scissors so that the head of the screw faces the paper, that is, towards your body.

The screw must be somewhat loose. If it is too tight, more force is required to cut and your hand and arm can become cramped, especially if you work for a long time. A looser screw makes the work considerably easier. You can use a fine screw driver to adjust the screw.

The Paper

Only the best quality paper is suitable for scherenschnitte. Poor-quality paper makes the work difficult. In general, long-fibered paper, which is strong and will not tear easily, is the easiest and best to work with. It is important that the paper not fade or discolor; use rag-content white paper that is acid-free (it won't yellow), or colored paper that will not fade. Recycled paper is very difficult to use because the fibers are too short, so making fine scherenschnitte from recycled paper is very demanding. Sometimes you have to choose lower-quality paper because the desired color is not available in a good quality.

Choose heavy or light paper according to your taste. I prefer heavy, dark black paper over all other types for free-cut scherenschnitte. For folded cutwork, a finer paper is more suitable. Gummed paper—that is, paper covered with glue—is not suitable because it often has a brittle coating that can crack when it is folded or unfolded, and then flake off.

For our purposes, we can distinguish among several major categories of paper:

- solid black or brown paper (of various thicknesses, matte or glossy)
- paper that is white and coated with a layer of black or brown on one side (matte or glossy)
- gummed paper
- white paper
- colored paper
- paper that you have colored yourself
- colored paper from brochures

The choice of paper is a matter of taste, but keep in mind that heavy paper is more suited for open cutting while lightweight paper is better for folded cutwork. Coated paper, which is white on the reverse side from where you will work, is easier on the eyes and easier to draw on. In contrast, on very black paper, you need to draw with a white pen, and your eyes will get tired when cutting it. A disadvantage of paper coated with black is that cutting from the back (white) side results in the white cut edges showing on the front (black) side. By cutting from the black front side, the cut edges remain black. White cut edges can have a disturbing effect on a black surface but are hardly visible if the scherenschnitte is glued to a white background. However, if the scherenschnitte is to be pasted onto colored paper, it is better to cut from the black front side and avoid any white showing.

Also, inexact cutting on coated paper can have a negative effect. In no case should you pull out any unevenly cut places, because the white fibers will show. It's better to cut these places over again carefully (see also Chapter 2, page 25).

You can color white paper yourself with wood stain. First test it with the scissors and judge whether it suits your purposes. The colors are available in powdered form. Mix them with mentholated spirits so that they don't run later if they come in contact with wet hands or drops of water. Take care when handling flammable spirits! The dissolved color is applied in several coats with a paintbrush or a cotton ball until you get the desired intensity. Irregularly colored paper can be attractive. Paper becomes firmer and stiffer when color is applied.

Colored paper is available in the quality used for origami, the Japanese art of folding paper. It is lightweight paper with intense colors and is excellent for folding and cutting.

Gilded paper can be very effective in decorations. However, it is expensive and, in addition, the blades of your scissors will suffer from cutting the metal, even if the layer of gold is extremely thin.

The techniques presented in this book are shown mainly using black paper, but you can use

Fig. 1.3 Scherenschnitte of Noah's Ark by the author.

most of the techniques with other types of paper as well—with colored paper, for example.

Background Paper

The paper onto which you paste the scheren-schnitte is very important. Rag-content paper, which will not turn yellow when exposed to sunlight, is best. Handmade paper is very suit-able and absorbs the glue well. Stark white paper, such as typing paper, results in too strong a contrast to the black scherenschnitte paper. A lightly tinted, eggshell-colored paper has a soft-er effect.

If you use colored paper as a background, be very careful when gluing; otherwise, the white glue will be visible after it is dry.

Cloth—silk, for example—can be used as a background. Be careful when gluing: watery glue can run along the fibers and form ugly flecks.

The Craft Knife

Certain cuttings are done more easily and clean-ly with a craft knife (also called a Japan knife) than with scissors. Round cutters, shaped like ballpoint pens, are very handy (Fig. 1.4). They are easier to work with and more precise to con-trol than a flat craft knife, making them good for long, straight cuts. Often each blade must be individually inserted in round craft knives. Make sure that the blades are always absolutely point-ed and sharp.

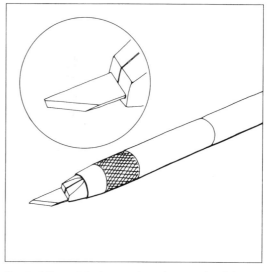

Fig. 1.4 The craft knife must always be pointed and sharp. A broken point is shown in the inset picture.

With use, the point can become flat because it has broken off, or round because it has been worn down.

A scalpel, such as those used by surgeons, can be used in place of a craft knife. The advantage is that you can sharpen the blades yourself; the disadvantage is the high price.

When using a craft knife for cutting, the pad on which you work is very important. If you use a cutting mat or rough cardboard, the point of the knife will become dull very quickly. Old photos, post cards, or fine cardboard are very suitable. A colored base makes the work easier because you quickly see what has already been cut out. Make sure there is a firm surface under the pad. Don't

use folded newspaper because the entire work could shift, and the craft knife would not be in the exact position required.

More about craft knives appears in Chapter 6. Working with a craft knife is often a matter of personal preference. Some people can work very well with them; others don't care for them at all. In all cases, be sure that the blade of the craft knife is very sharp. This tool is less suitable for children.

The Work Place

Scherenschnitte can actually be done anywhere and does not require any special setup. The only necessity is good light, and daylight is clearly preferable. Halogen lamps are very good, but they must be aimed directly at the work. In addition, it is important to sit in a comfortable and relaxed way. On page 26 you can see the proper posture for cutting.

2. The Basics of Cutting

Creating scherenschnitte is fun from the start, and even the first attempts of adults or children produce good results. If you read this chapter first and follow the tips given in it, you can avoid many unhappy mistakes.

Copying and Sketching

Copying motifs can be a good technique, especially in the beginning. Don't hesitate to learn from existing designs that please you. You can concentrate entirely on practicing by cutting various scherenschnitte shapes that have different levels of difficulty. For each of the techniques described in the following chapters, you will find a large number of practice examples suitable for copying.

With time, if you master the technical skills, you'll want to create your own designs and shapes. In the beginning, when you have limited experience, it's advisable to copy the designs exactly. As your ability in the technique advances and with increasing experience in design, you won't need to copy every detail any longer. It will be sufficient just to sketch your idea in rough outline. Begin to free yourself from the original and let your fantasy roam.

You will need carbon paper to transfer the original design onto the white side of the scherenschnitte paper. When choosing carbon paper be sure that the color doesn't come off too easily and cause the drawing to get smeared from being touched or moved. And it's fairly unpleas-

ant when your hands turn black.

Secure the three layers of paper (scherenschnitte paper—carbon paper—original, Fig. 2.1) with transparent tape or paper clips, so that they don't shift. Then with a sharp, hard pencil, draw along the contours of the original. If you're taking the design from a book, first make a photocopy and work from that. Or you can trace the original onto a somewhat transparent but not too thick piece of paper, and then use that as the original for copying onto the scherenschnitte paper.

To copy for the folded cutwork technique, the original must first be folded exactly down the middle. Then, together with the carbon paper,

Fig. 2.1 For copying designs, securely fasten the three layers of paper together; on the bottom, the scherenschnitte paper with the white side up; in the middle, the carbon paper; on top, the original.

the folded original is wrapped around the folded scherenschnitte paper (Fig. 2.2).

If you want to copy writing, be careful that there are no enclosed areas that will not show up later. Letters and numbers that you want to appear positive (i.e., dark figures on a light background) must always be contiguous with the edge of the paper. In contrast, with negative characters (light figures on a dark background) you have to work with enclosed areas that will be left out (Fig. 2.3). Remember that the letters and numbers must always be drawn on the back side of the paper. This is easier if you place the three layers of paper in a different order: on the very bottom, the carbon paper with the colored side facing up; in the middle, the scherenschnitte paper with the white side facing down;

and on top, the normal original. In this way, the drawing will come out reversed on the white side of the scherenschnitte paper.

When copying any design, you must consider copyright laws. If you want to use copyrighted works for more than home use, you absolutely must get permission.

Over time, try to get away from copying; make your own designs and even try to develop your own style. Take the time in the beginning to make exact drawings of your concepts in advance. Don't become discouraged if your first project falls into pieces after you cut it (Fig. 2.4). To avoid this mistake, pay attention from the start to the necessary connecting points and try to imagine the finished cut lines. Designing for folded cutwork can be difficult, especially in

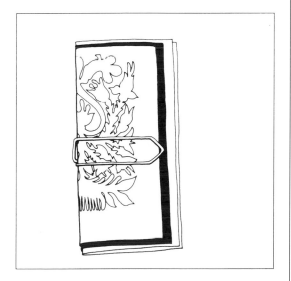

Fig. 2.2 For folded cutwork, both the original and the carbon paper are folded and wrapped around the scherenschnitte paper.

Fig. 2.3 Letters and numbers must be drawn reversed. A simple method is described in the text.

the beginning: tree trunks become thick pillars, or the distances between different parts will turn into large holes. Keep in mind that the areas in the middle double in size. Pay careful attention to the correct side when copying and drawing.

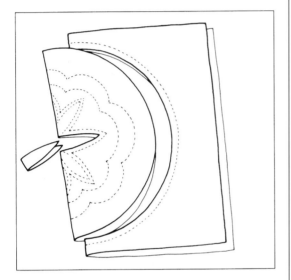

Fig. 2.4 In the example, the individual sections fall apart because they are not connected anywhere.

For example, if a building is to appear authentic on a scherenschnitte, it will have to be drawn or copied from the reverse side beforehand. The same problem arises when designing a sequence in a certain order, such as the succession of the seasons. If designs such as these are to be used, the original must first be copied and then a new original placed reversed on the carbon paper.

Basic Rules of Cutting

If the subject is drawn clearly and exactly so that nothing can be misunderstood when cutting, then you can begin. Right-handed people should always begin from the bottom right; it is better for left-handed people to begin at the bottom left (Fig. 2.5). Cut exactly along the drawn line and be careful to cut continuously and without removing the scissors. Don't leave out the difficult spots to come back to cut later. In no case should you start at intersecting

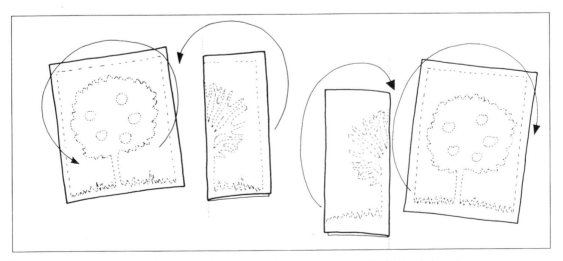

Fig. 2.5 Left: direction of cutting for right-handed people. Right: direction of cutting for left-handed people.

points, because the paper will lose its stability and become difficult to guide. Use the entire cutting surface of the scissors, not just the tip. The right hand with the scissors remains steady (Fig. 2.6–2.8); only the left hand moves and

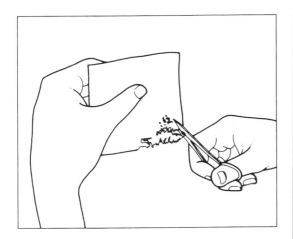

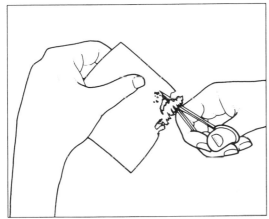

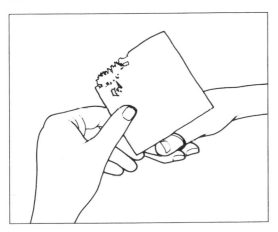

Fig. 2.6-2.8 The hand with the scissors does not move, while the other hand directs the paper into the scissors.

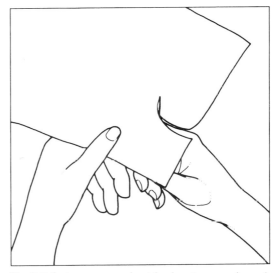

Fig. 2.9 Cutting a curve to the right: the scissors are beneath the paper.

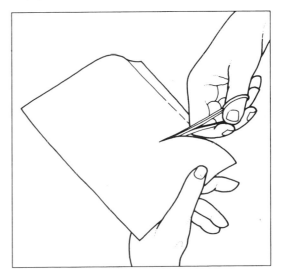

Fig. 2.10 Cutting a curve to the left: the scissors are above the paper.

guides the paper into the scissors so that the desired shape results. For left-handed people the opposite is true: hold the left hand with the scissors steady and move the right. Cutting is considerably easier if the scissors are guided beneath the paper when making a right curve (Fig. 2.9) and above the paper when making a left curve (Fig. 2.10). When cutting very fine details, the scissors may rest on two fingers of the hand that is holding the paper. In this way the cutting hand remains steady (Fig. 2.11). Take care that no jagged places result. Jagged edges occur when one cut does not continue on exactly from the last (Fig. 2.12 and 2.13). You can eliminate these mistakes with practice.

A basic rule for the sequence of the cutting is to first cut the areas in the middle of the work, then on the edge, and finally along the outline.

In this way, the stability of the paper is maintained for the longest possible time, and guiding the paper and the scissors is much easier.

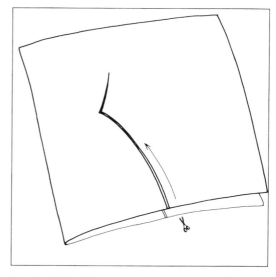

Fig. 2.12 Guide the scissors without stopping. A clean cut will result.

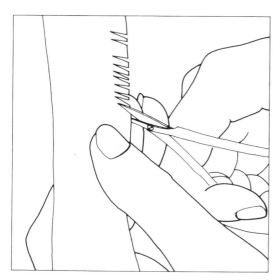

Fig. 2.11 For fine details, rest the scissors on the hand holding the paper

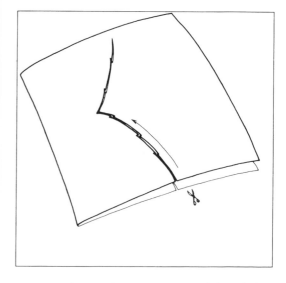

Fig. 2.13 If one cut does not continue exactly from the last, unattractive jagged lines will result.

These basic rules apply to all techniques. Sometimes, however, there are reasons to deviate from this sequence. In these cases the ideal sequence of steps for each of the techniques is described individually. In the chapter "Folded Cutwork" you will find practice examples with the exact sequence of cutting.

For enclosed areas, pierce the middle of the surface with the tip of the scissors (Fig. 2.14- 2.16) or with a needle. Lay cardboard under the original before using a needle. Starting from the pierced point, cut to the edge of the surface and continue counter-clockwise (left-handed people clockwise) until the entire surface is cut. You need very sharp scissors for this; otherwise, the hole will not be clean. For effortless cutting, it is best to cut away the falling portions continuously, so that your work can continue unhindered.

If the work has not turned out nicely enough, in many cases it can be cut over again cleanly. However, there is a problem with figures if the

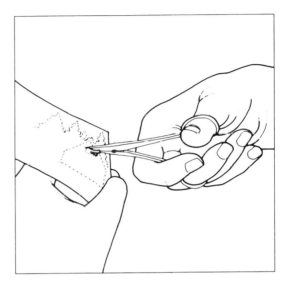

Fig. 2.15 Cutting from the middle to the edge. Right-handed people cut the enclosed area counter-clockwise; left-handed people clockwise.

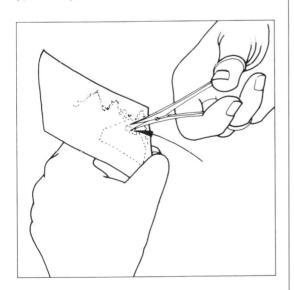

Fig. 2.14 Pierce the middle of the enclosed area with the tip of the scissors.

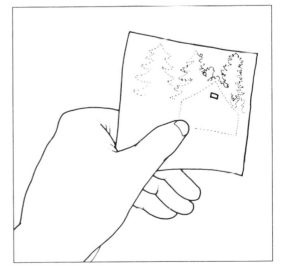

Fig. 2.16 When the enclosed areas in the middle are cut, then you may begin with the outer lines.

face has not turned out as well as desired. Cut off the head and replace it with a newly cut one if it cannot be salvaged at all. For a time it was considered very important that a scherenschnitte be cut from one piece of paper. In earlier times, however, many artists created their scherenschnitte in several sections, which could be very attractive.

Be careful never to let the scissors fall, even onto the table. The tip is extremely sensitive. If the tip or the cutting edges get damaged, they can be repaired by a professional, provided the scissors are made of top-quality steel. The scissors will get shorter with grinding.

You will save a lot of time if you have a frame on hand before beginning your work. It is often very difficult to find a suitable frame afterwards, and it is costly to have a frame made to measure. If possible, select the format of your scherenschnitte according to the frame that you have. Additional information about frames can be found in Chapter 10.

Pay attention to your posture while cutting and try to remain relaxed in the back of your neck and shoulders. In the beginning, because they are concentrating hard, many people make the mistake of holding the scissors and paper higher and higher. Propping up your elbows can help keep the back of your neck and shoulder areas relaxed. A good working posture results from keeping your upper arms close to the upper body (Fig. 2.17).

For larger projects it is wise to pay attention to your clothes: avoid wearing pullovers with wide

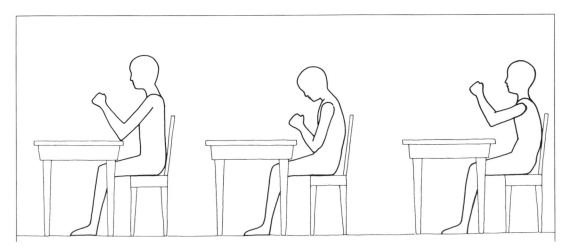

Fig. 2.17 Correct posture left and in the middle: Supported elbows help to keep the back of the neck and shoulders relaxed. The upper arms are kept close to the body. Wrong posture on the right: the arms and the scherenschnitte are too high.

sleeves, because areas that have been cut can easily get caught in the fibers of a sweater. If that happens, don't tug at them but try to free them carefully.

The following chapter describes the first technique, folded cutwork, and repeats the basic rules, because many things are more easily understood when explained in connection with a concrete example. For that reason, the simple

practice examples for folding and cutting are very detailed, so it is advisable—especially for beginners—to study the technique first. Most of what is explained there can be applied to other techniques. The chapter on free-form scherenschnitte has a wealth of examples and designs that you can use to practice. The many possibilities for practice in these two chapters offer a good basis for applying other techniques and beginning to work with your own designs.

3. FOLDED CUTWORK

Perhaps the first thing we think of when we hear about scherenschnitte is folding and cutting colored paper, which most of us have probably done as children. Actually, astonishing effects can be created this way. Very simple motifs have a much greater effect when the design is multiplied when unfolded. We can fold the paper just once—this is known as simple folded cutwork—or we can fold it several times and get multiple folded cutwork.

Fig. 3.1 This example shows clearly that the sketch did not take into consideration the result of unfolding, which doubled the thickness of the tree trunk: the trunk is too massive in comparison to the crown of the tree.

Simple Folded Cutwork

For cutting folded paper, it is better to use stronger scissors and a finer quality of paper. Fold the paper so that the black side is on the inside and the fold to the left. Left-handed people should have the fold in front of them on the right. The creases should be folded very carefully and exactly. Because you see only half of it when it is folded, be careful not to make the drawing of the middle area too massive. Try to imagine how the scherenschnitte will look when it is unfolded (Fig. 3.1 and 3.2).

Before sketching the design, secure the edges with paper clips or tape or sew it on a sewing

Fig. 3.2 Here, in contrast, is a well-proportioned tree trunk and crown.

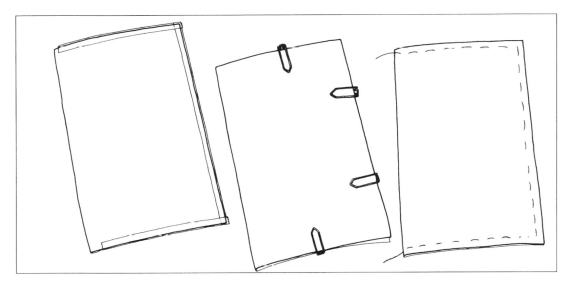

Fig. 3.3 Before making the drawing, the folded paper should be secured carefully with transparent tape, paper clips, or by sewing.

machine (Fig. 3.3) to prevent the layers of paper from shifting. Don't open the scherenschnitte until it is completely cut. It can often be very difficult to place the two parts together again exactly after they are cut.

Practice Exercises

The examples have been chosen so that they gradually increase in difficulty, and each step is practiced several times before moving on to the next one. What follows is the basic sequence of steps: begin by first cutting areas along the fold, then the inner areas. When cutting enclosed inner areas, proceed as described and illustrated in Chapter 2, page 25. Only after those are finished should you go on to the outer edges. You will find instructions for left-handed and right-handed people in the following examples. This

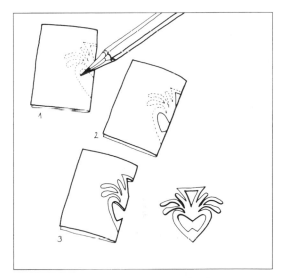

Fig. 3.4 Practice example for left-handed people: the fold is on the right. After drawing the design (1) cut along the lines near the fold (2) then along the outer contours.

way, the basic principle, which was illustrated in Chapter 2, will be shown in a concrete fashion

Fig. 3.5 Practice example for right-handed people. The fold is to the left. Sequence of cutting: areas at the fold (1), outer lines (2).

Fig. 3.7 Sequence of cutting (for left-handed people): areas along the fold (1), inner lines (2), outer lines (3).

Fig. 3.6 Sequence of cutting (for right-handed people), as in Fig. 3.5.

Fig. 3.8 Sequence of cutting (for right-handed people), as in Fig. 3.7.

and practiced in several examples. These basic rules hold for all techniques and won't be explained each time unless special cases arise.

In this chapter I introduce the cutting of points. While the procedure shown here does not apply to folded cutwork, it can be used for most of

Fig. 3.9 Sequence of cutting (for right-handed people), as in Fig. 3./

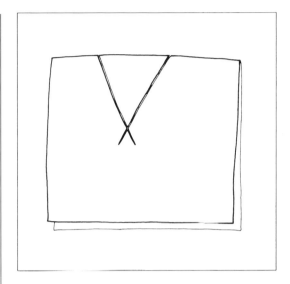

Fig. 3.10 Avoid overlapping cuts.

the other techniques. Basically, we can distinguish between sharp and soft points. These two types are cut differently.

To make a sharp point, the scissors are applied twice. Cut out both sides of the triangle, being careful not to cut too deeply at the point. The overlapping area is very visible after unfolding (Fig. 3.10). If you cut carefully, you should be able to feel with the scissors when you reach the place where the first cut ended, because at that point the resistance stops. Likewise you should avoid cutting too little, because then the point will not come out well. If you tear out the points, the white paper fibers will be visible (Fig. 3.11). When cutting points at an outer edge, the usual sequence is changed somewhat. In this case, cut the outer edge first; then you can cut the finest points easily (Fig. 3.12).

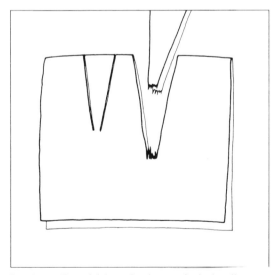

Fig. 3.11 If you didn't cut deeply enough, don't pull out the point, because the white paper fibers will become visible.

The following procedure works best for points at the edge of an inner area: first cut a continuous line to which all the points lead (Fig. 3.13, first cut). You can then cut the individual points easi-

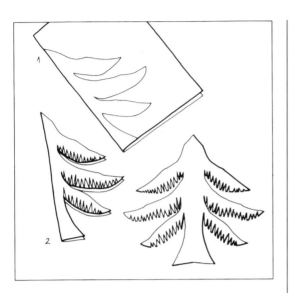

Fig. 3.12 When cutting points at an outer edge, the usual sequence will be altered somewhat. For the fir tree, first cut the outer edge, then you'll be able to cut the finest points without any difficulty.

Fig. 3.13 Points on the edge of inside areas. Sequence of cutting: areas along the fold and a continuous line at which the points will end (1); proceeding from this line you can easily cut the tips (2). As usual, outer lines last (3).

Fig. 3.14 Sequence of cutting, as in Fig. 3.13

ly, continuing from this cut line. The distribution of the points and possible variations are shown in Figures 3.15 to 3.19. Sharp points can be cut with a craft knife (compare Chapter 6). Soft points appear more natural for grass or twigs. This technique is completely different, because it's important this time not to remove the scissors. Make the first cut deep enough to create the grass, for example, as desired. Then turn the

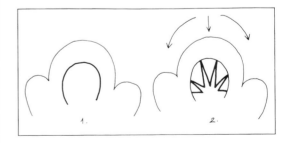

Fig. 3.15 To achieve a good distribution of points, begin in the middle.

Fig. 3.16 Poorly distributed points.

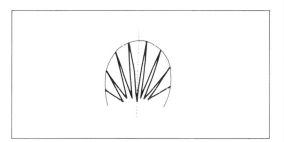

Fig. 3.17 A good distribution of points.

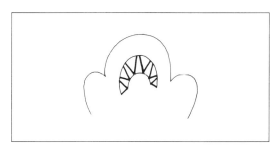

Fig. 3.18 Blunt points appear to be connected to the edge.

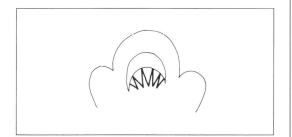

Fig. 3.19 A distinctive effect results by directing the points downward, after first cutting out a crescent-shaped area.

paper and cut upward again, without removing the scissors, make a turn, and then cut downward again (Fig. 3.20 and 3.21).

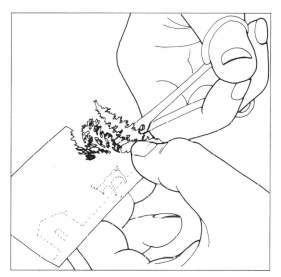

Fig. 3.20 Soft points: the first cut determines the depth of the point.

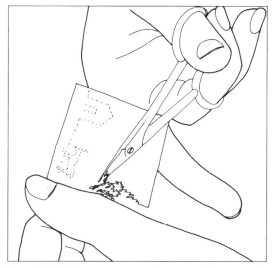

Fig. 3.21 Without stopping, turn the paper and cut upward again, then down again.

For wreath shapes, which are especially nice when you are making greeting cards, it is better if you change the usual sequence of cutting somewhat. Cut the large inner area last, because otherwise the paper will lose its stability and no longer be easy to guide.

After cutting, unfolding the sheet and making more cuts can result in an even more attractive piece. The folded cutwork shown at the beginning of this chapter had elements added after being unfolded. The procedure is very easy. After finishing the cuts on the folded paper, unfold the cutting, draw more designs on the back, and cut them out.

On the following pages you'll find a large number of simple examples, as well as more difficult ones, on which you can practice. Use the techniques described above or make variations if you wish. Give your fantasy free rein and begin to make your own designs.

42

Multiple Folded Cutwork

While simple folded cutwork achieves its effect because the subject is doubled, multiple folded cutwork, as the name implies, does so by multiplying the motifs. It is precisely this multiplication that results in astonishing effects, and simple motifs can achieve an even greater impact in this way. For that reason, easy multiple folded cutwork is especially suitable for children. It is made by folding a square, rectangle, or circle several times. Figures 3.22 and 3.23 show how paper can be folded.

Be very careful when folding the paper, and the more times it is folded, the more careful you must be. The paper layers can shift very easily when they are being cut; therefore it is important to secure the paper well. If the paper is to be folded several times, it is best to use fine paper and a very stable pair of scissors. Be very careful when unfolding the paper. The parts stick to one another and can tear easily if you pull too hard.

The four multiple folded cuttings on page 47 (right column) and 48 were all made by Christa Bachmann, scherenschnitte artist and prize winner, whose work is in the tradition of the folded cuttings typical of the Ore Mountains in eastern Germany.

Fig. 3.22 Possible ways of folding. The types of folding shown here can be changed, of course, by folding along additional axes.

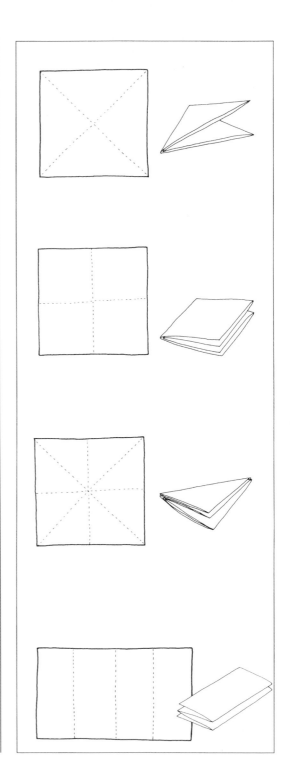

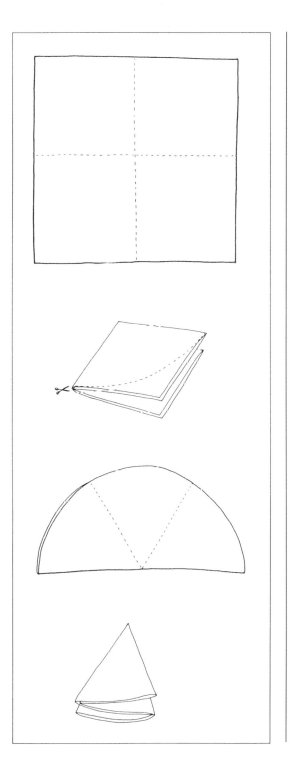

Fig. 3.23 A special type of folding that results in a scherenschnitte with six axes. An example is the scherenschnitte with the fir trees in the middle of page 49.

4. Free-form or Open Cutting

As far as technique is concerned, there are no
unusual features in free-form scherenschnitte.
The tips given in Chapter 2, "The Basics of
Cutting," are important and valid for this type as
well. Pay special attention to the rule not to
begin cutting at different places. Continue cutting wherever you begin, because if you cut at
different places, the paper loses its stability and
can no longer be successfully guided.

5. Scherenschnitte with Borders

Scherenschnitte with borders can be made using various techniques. There are only a few special features when cutting.

The following procedure works best (Fig. 5.1-5.3): Choose the size of the scherenschnitte and make a drawing. First cut the inner, enclosed areas with a craft knife or scissors. Ideally you should begin by cutting the inside of the border, leaving the outer edge uncut. Cut the entire inner area of the scherenschnitte first before

Fig. 5.2 First cut all the small inner areas.

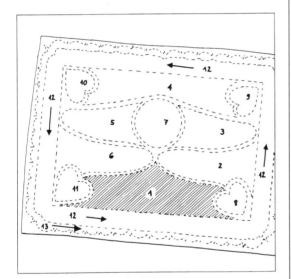

Fig. 5.1 It is important to plan the work for a large scherenschnitte with a border. This overview shows the sequence in which the areas must be worked. Begin with the areas inside. First the large inner areas (1–7) in a counter-clockwise direction (left-handed people clockwise), then the small inner areas (8–11). When the inner areas of the scherenschnitte are completely finished, then work on the border (12). The outer contours come last (13).

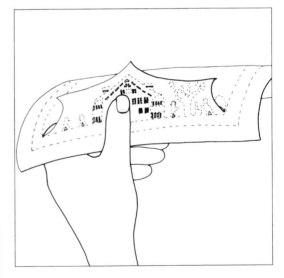

Fig. 5.3 Begin in area 1 as follows: Cut the uppermost line of the section with the first cut, thereby opening the paper. Then the large remaining part of the paper can easily be pushed back and will not interfere with the work.

working on the border. This keeps the paper stable as long as possible and allows it to be guided easily. After the inner section is cut, continue cutting out the enclosed areas in the border. Finally, work the outer edge of the border.

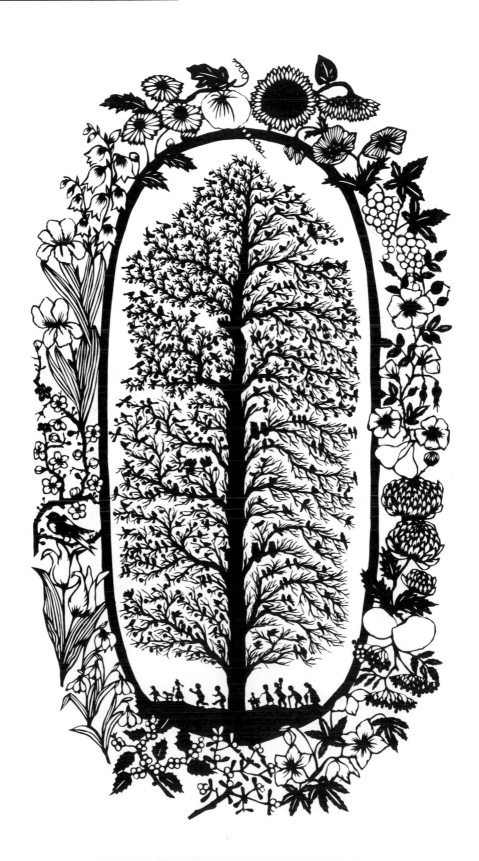

6. Cutting with a Craft Knife

The first chapter dealt briefly with the craft knife as a working tool. You might want to review that section and read this one as well before you begin to cut.

Always guide the craft knife straight ahead; avoid putting any pressure on the side, as the blade could quickly break off. Don't hold the craft knife vertically; it cuts better when it is held like a pencil. Check the point often, because as soon as it is damaged or no longer sharp, the paper will not be cut but torn. Be careful not to apply too much pressure on the blade, as it will sink into the cardboard and you will be unable to see the length of the cut (Fig. 6.1).

Always guide the craft knife towards yourself when cutting. This holds for rounded contours or circles: begin with the first cut at the upper middle and guide it downward. Then place the craft knife in the upper middle again and cut the other half of the circle. (Fig. 6.2)

If you wish to use the craft knife to cut out small areas that are close together, stretch and hold the paper with the fingers of your free hand (Fig. 6.3) to prevent creases from forming in the paper and to ensure correct cutting. If the paper is not smooth and tight, the paper will probably tear.

People whose hands tremble easily can achieve good results with the craft knife because the pressure stops the trembling.

The craft knife is better suited than scissors for certain structures or motifs. Among those are birds' feathers, decorations on borders, and the great variety of eyes (Fig. 6.4).

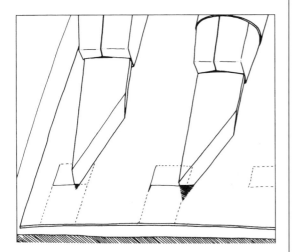

Fig. 6.1 Pressure that is too heavy pushes the craft knife into the cardboard and the cut will be too long (right). By applying lighter pressure, the cut remains shorter and easier to control (left).

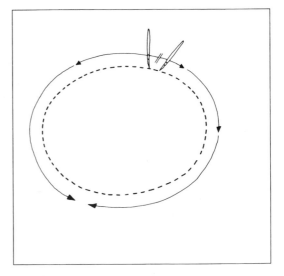

Fig. 6.2 Circles are cut in two steps with the craft knife. Always cut towards yourself.

Frequently, work consisting of numerous small or very tiny cuts is very time-consuming. However, these patterns achieve a fascinating effect. The following practice exercises are designed to illustrate this technique.

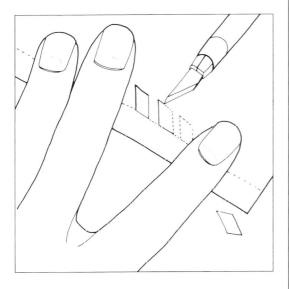

Fig. 6.3 The paper must be stretched tightly with one hand when making small cuts with the craft knife.

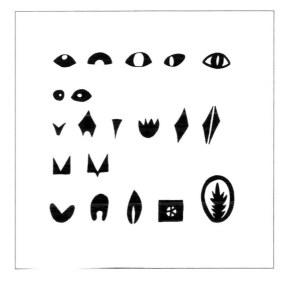

Fig. 6.4 Patterns that are especially suited for the craft knife—for example, eyes and feathers. Detailed eyes always look better than simple holes (above).

7. Positive-Negative Cutwork

The name of this chapter indicates what is special about this technique. Two scherenschnitte are made from one piece of paper and from a single cutting: a positive cutting, and a negative cutting that results from what is cut away. The positive cutting has the effect of a day cutting and the negative cutting functions as a night cutting. Concentration and precise cutting will ensure that no mistake endangers the negative cutting (the cut-away section). Therefore you need to draw the design clearly and exactly. Avoid closed areas, because they will fall out of the cut piece and will be missing from the negative cutting. When cutting, concentrate on not cutting anything away entirely, either from the positive or the negative part. When designing

the cutting, pay close attention to the balance of dark and light. Too much light color quickly creates a dull effect, while too much darkness can have a heavy effect.

This technique is very demanding because it allows for no mistakes at all. Perhaps for this reason it is not very widespread. Fig. 7.1 shows an example from around 1700. The scherenschnitte is shown in its original size.

Fig. 7.2 demonstrates a playful variation of the positive-negative effect. The scherenschnitte artist Adolf Menzel (1815-1905) cut a head from white paper and created the positive black head by casting its shadow on a wall.

Fig. 7.1 Christ in Gethsemane, original size (ca. 1700).

Fig. 7.2 Scherenschnitte by Adolf Menzel (1815-1905). The head shown above was cut from white paper. The positive shown below was created by holding the scherenschnitte between the light and the wall.

92

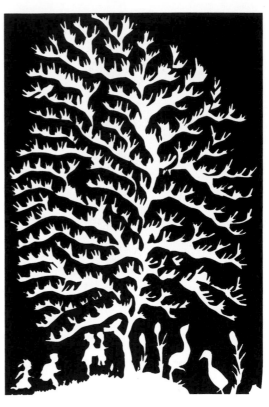

8. Colored Scherenschnitte

There are many ways to design colored scheren-schnitte, so your imagination need have no limits. The variants shown here are meant to inspire you to independent experimentation. When choosing the paper, be sure that it is light-fast. You don't want your scherenschnitte to fade. Obtain some colored origami paper and proceed exactly as with black scherenschnitte. When working with light colors, be careful to draw very fine lines and to draw very precisely. Thick lines will cause the sketch to be visible on the right side. A precisely drawn sketch cut exactly along the lines will pro-duce a scherenschnitte to be proud of. It is better to cut a little inside the line so that the pencil marks are completely cut away.

To add another element, several scherenschnitte in complementary or contrasting colors can be cut and glued together, in layers one behind the other. In this case, it's good to have an idea of the desired final product before beginning to cut the first color, so that the distribution of space, color, and proportions will be easier.

An effective variation is the combination of black paper with light or dark grey that conjures up attractive suggestions of fog.

The following technique provides playful vari-ety: cut many individual parts of a design from different colored papers, arrange them, and then glue them together like a collage. When gluing, work carefully, because white glue is slightly vis-ible on a colored background. This method is a lot of fun but does require some care when choosing the colors so that the final product does not look too gaudy. Pay close attention to the proportions.

If you want to add a layer of another color to existing cut paper, first lay some transparent paper on the motif to be used and, using a pen-cil, copy the desired outline in the correct size to produce the pattern for cutting the colored paper. With increasing practice your sense of proportion will become better and you will not need cutting patterns any longer. Beautiful examples of this technique are the traditional Polish scherenschnitte. Examples of them appear on page 137.

Colored paper can be placed beneath the scherenschnitte, used not only as background paper on which to glue the scherenschnitte but as a colorful element of the design. Individual parts of the scherenschnitte—butterfly wings, for example—can be placed on particular colors. The colored surfaces that result give the scherenschnitte a very special appearance. This is a very demanding technique and requires very exacting work. In China, colorful scheren-schnitte such as those described here are very common.

To decorate scherenschnitte and give it a more elegant appearance, you can cut small pieces of gold leaf and glue them on to appropriate motifs (for example, butterflies, fish, and stars). Color the paper yourself and create your own palette of colors to make attractive pieces.

Techniques for painting with wood stain or watercolors are described in Chapter One, page 15. In this way you are independent of conventional colored paper and have the chance of working with the exact nuances of colors that you desire. Coloring or painting the scherenschnitte after it is finished is a technique frequently used in China. The dragon on page 119 has been made in this way.

Because this book shows mainly black scherenschnitte, let me mention white cutwork, for the sake of completeness. It is even older than black scherenschnitte. Information of interest about the history of white cutwork and further examples are in the last chapter on page 121. Be especially careful when drawing on and gluing white cutwork, because white, often transparent, paper does not allow for many mistakes. White cutwork is ideal for winter landscapes with snow and ice; they can express bone-rattling cold wonderfully well.

Susanne Schläpfer-Geiser

9. SCHERENSCHNITTE ON EGGS

Decorating eggs is an old fascination with a long tradition. Scherenschnitte on eggs is only one possibility for the various techniques. Before you can begin to decorate eggs with scherenschnitte, the eggs have to be carefully prepared.

Preparing the Eggs

The selection of the eggs is important; only perfect eggs—that is, those without bits of calcium on the shell or other irregularities—will do. Eggs with thin shells are not suitable either. After carefully selecting the egg and washing it, make a small hole in the tip. Because it is needed only for blowing air out, the hole can be very small; you can make it with a fine four-cornered

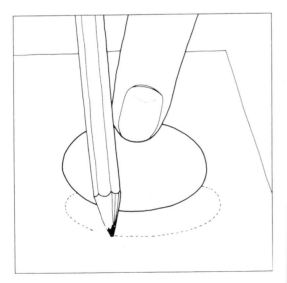

Fig. 9.1 Measure each egg before drawing a design.

drill. Drill a somewhat larger hole in the bottom (round) end of the egg. Stick a needle into this hole so the skin of the egg is pierced and stir the contents of the egg well. It is important that the edges of the holes are smooth and not broken. Then blow out the egg with a rubber pump (available in stores). Rinse out the egg and dry it carefully. None of the contents should remain; otherwise, mites could develop inside and damage the decorated egg.

Wallpaper Paste

Fix the finished scherenschnitte onto the egg with paste. Mixed with water, a teaspoonful of wallpaper paste powder yields a small jar of paste. A tightly covered jar of paste will keep for a long time (up to a year) in the refrigerator. If the paste is too thin, the scherenschnitte could separate from the egg after drying. On the other hand, if the paste is too thick, it will form lumps. If this happens, thin it with some water.

The Scherenschnitte

Measure the prepared egg: lay the egg on the back side of the paper you have chosen. Draw the contours of the egg with a pencil (Fig. 9.1). Every egg has its own individual shape. It can be oblong or round as a ball, fat or thin, large or small. Measuring before drawing helps to ensure that the scherenschnitte will fit on the egg. Draw on the measured paper surface, then cut out the scherenschnitte. Cut the enclosed areas first, then the outer lines.

It is best to paste a scherenschnitte on both the front and back sides of the egg, or you could use a border to decorate around the egg.

Then coat the clean egg with a thin layer of paste where the scherenschnitte is to be placed. The simplest way of doing this is with your finger. Lay the scherenschnitte on the egg. The position can be corrected with a craft knife before the paper gets soft from the paste and sticks to the rounded surfaces of the egg. When the scherenschnitte is in the proper position, the excess paste can be wiped off with a paper towel. Be careful: if paste gets on the paper, it will leave unattractive spots. Don't rub the scherenschnitte because it is still very fragile.

When everything is thoroughly dry, you can spray the egg with clear varnish to protect it. To do that, place the egg on a wooden stick, which could be anchored in a Styrofoam plate. The egg must not be touched until it is completely finished and dry. Use varnish only sparingly so that no drops form underneath the egg.

White cutwork on brown eggs looks very attractive, but the white paper loses the intensity of its color when it's treated with varnish and then can't be seen very well. There is an advantage to not varnishing the egg: if the decorated egg breaks, the pieces, including the scherenschnitte, can be placed in water; the scherenschnitte will come off the shell after a while and can be used again if handled carefully.

If you wish to hang the egg on a ribbon, make the upper hole somewhat larger. Attach the ribbon to a piece of toothpick or a match. Insert the little piece of wood into the hole and place it sideways. Then you can hang up the egg. The hole must be drilled exactly in the middle in this case, otherwise the egg will not hang straight.

Eggs can be decorated with black or colored scherenschnitte. A collage technique with its many colors offers several possibilities as well. The light-fastness of the paper is less important for this because the eggs probably will be exposed to light only on special occasions.

10. Finishing Touches

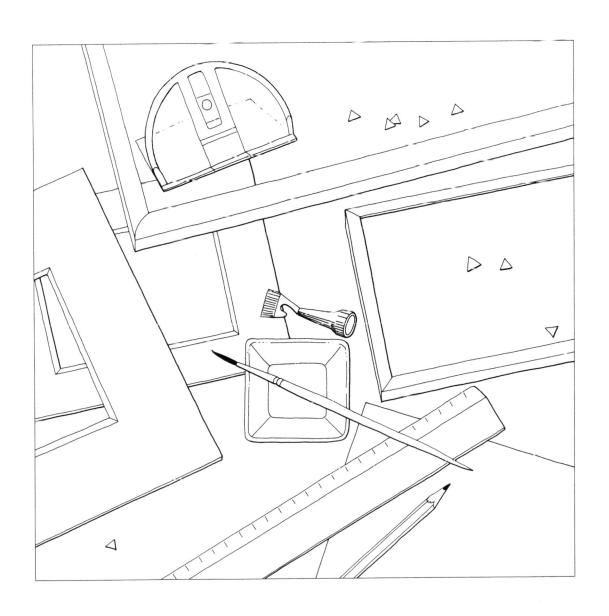

Gluing Scherenschnitte

If scherenschnitte is to be glued, take care to use good, acid-free paper for the background. It would be a shame if the background got yellow quickly after so much work. Typing paper is not a good choice. Lightly tinted paper, which has a softer effect than stark white, is preferable. Handmade paper with its special texture can be very effective.

If the paper is thin and large in size, it can easily get creased due to the moisture in the glue. Therefore, a basic principle is the larger the surface, the heavier the paper.

If you are working with a scherenschnitte that is to be attached to a card, an egg, or a wooden object, it must be pasted on completely. If the work of art is to be placed behind glass, it is sufficient to paste it lightly at several spots, but it is advisable to at least partially paste it to prevent shifting.

Before you begin pasting, smooth the scherenschnitte with an iron. Heat the iron only slightly so that it doesn't turn the paper brown, and don't use any steam. Iron it on top of a piece of cardboard with the black or colored side down. You'll immediately notice if a part has been folded under. Just press with the iron; do not under any circumstances rub with it. Pasting is much easier after working with an iron, especially on large pieces of scherenschnitte.

Now place the scherenschnitte exactly on the place where you wish to paste it and mark lightly with a pencil. Measuring and centering the scherenschnitte is especially important with a large piece and for work that consists mainly of borders, that is, a design with a open inner area. Irregularities in these types are very noticeable, and once a scherenschnitte has been pasted on, it cannot be moved again.

For pasting use water-soluble white glue that has been thinned by half with water. Avoid using glue that forms threads or that is glossy after drying.

The thinned white glue is best placed in a small, flat dish to the right of your work (for left-handed people on the left side). Take up a small amount of glue with a clean, fine paintbrush and remove any excess. Apply some glue on the background paper at a place that seems suitable.

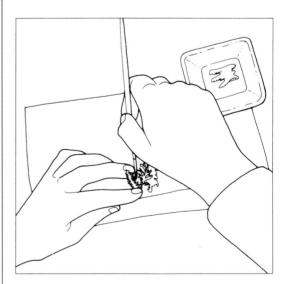

Fig. 10.1 Gluing the scherenschnitte

With your free hand, hold the scherenschnitte firmly so that it does not move. (Fig. 10.1.)

Do not allow the glue to touch the black surface, because it will leave ugly whitish flecks. Press down with a paper towel on the glued places of the scherenschnitte until the glue begins to get firm. Continue in the same way until the entire object is glued. Never rub the surface but only dab it with a paper towel. Rubbing can cause the black surface to come off and lose its color.

It's not a good idea to cover an entire piece with glue at one time, because the paper can become soft and roll together. Very fine areas can get damaged very quickly, because wet paper tears easily. Handmade paper absorbs excess glue. In general, white background paper is easier to handle, because the white glue will not be visible on it. When using colored background paper, the glue must be applied very exactly where the scherenschnitte will be placed. Excess glue would be very visible. For very delicate parts, replace the paintbrush with a pin or toothpick. In any case, begin with the large areas and continue working until you reach the finest branches.

Gummed paper sticks too easily if your hands are wet. Spray glue is a problem with very fine or complicated cutwork, because the entire surface sticks at one time. If they are not glued exactly, it is almost impossible to remove delicate parts without damaging them. When using white glue, you can correct mistakes with a craft knife as long as the glue hasn't begun to harden.

Before placing the scherenschnitte in a frame, the glue must be thoroughly dry; otherwise the moisture from the glue will collect on the glass. Although paper can become very brittle when exposed to strong sunlight, scherenschnitte can be placed between two pieces of glass and hung in the window. In that case be especially careful to use light-fast paper. It is attractive if both sides of the paper are colored. The two pieces of glass can be soddered together with pieces of zinc and hung up like a coat of arms. (Check with a craft store that carries supplies for stained glass.)

When your work is finished, wash the paintbrush and dish as quickly as possible so that the glue doesn't dry. Otherwise you'll have to soak both items.

If you wish to paste the scherenschnitte onto wood, such as children's hangers or wooden boxes, for example, proceed in the same way as with eggs. Attach the scherenschnitte with wallpaper paste, and after it is dry apply several coats of varnish over the entire object so that the scherenschnitte won't be damaged with use.

Frames

Frames come in a variety of shapes and in different sizes and proportions. You can use oval, round, five- or six-sided frames, or square or rectangular shapes.

Ideally you should choose the frame before beginning the scherenschnitte, so you can fit your design to the available frame.

Often it's difficult to find a suitable frame afterward. Of course you could custom-make a frame yourself or have one made, but this can be time-consuming and costly.

The choice of frame is very important. As the idea for the scherenschnitte is developed, you should determine the approximate size and look around for a suitable frame. It should not only have the correct proportions but also suit the theme. For example, a rather rustic theme would not look good in a luxurious, elaborate frame. Ideally the frame should complement the scherenschnitte and reinforce its expression. Choose according to what seems right to you.

Fig. 10.2 An example of an unusual frame: an old window which now frames four scherenschnitte representing various fairy tales.

Take care when choosing the frame and preparing the scherenschnitte that enough space is left between the scherenschnitte and the frame. If the space is too small, the scherenschnitte loses its effect and appears cramped.

Wide frames can have a very decorative effect under certain conditions but, because they are too heavy in relationship to the scherenschnitte, they are really not suitable for smaller cutwork. Very narrow frames can create another difficulty. The upper edge of the frame might bend under the weight of a large scherenschnitte unless the mountings are placed at the extreme sides. The border lends a certain unity to the scherenschnitte. Borderless frames can allow dust to get in at the edges and affect the paper. If you have a frame made, you avoid all these possible sources of mistakes, but it can be expensive. If you do your own work, you need some practice and experience in order to get good results.

I do not recommend nonreflective glass. It takes away from the charm of scherenschnitte and makes it appear flat and lifeless. It gives the effect more of a print than a lively, structured work of paper art.

Matting

Matting is an additional framework of cardboard or heavy paper. The scherenschnitte is set off by the matting, creating a finished impression. You can use a single mat or several, one on top of the other. Several smaller windows cut out in the matting can be attractive.

You can cut matting yourself with a craft knife from heavy paper. If you cut your own matting, first measure the exact size, draw on the reverse side and then cut. Use a ruler to guide the cut and get an exactly straight line. In all cases, avoid cutting across intersections.

If you want a firmer matting, a specialty shop can cut one to order for you. Mat board comes in all colors, with layers of material, with contrasting colors in the inner part, and in all imaginable thicknesses, in sheets about 48 X 32 inches (120 X 80 cm). Buy only rag content matting, which will not yellow. Cutting heavy matting from cardboard yourself is not especially easy. Purchase a matting hand cutter with a diagonal blade, as shown in the illustration on page 111, top center, or a matting machine (very expensive). Be very sure that the blade is absolutely sharp and undamaged; otherwise, the uppermost layer of paper will be crushed instead of cut. For the best results when using a matting cutter or machine, use another piece of matting as a base on which to cut. It is especially important not to cut across any intersections and to cut the edges very carefully and exactly. Rough edges can be smoothed with emery paper if necessary, but this works only for very small corrections. It takes a lot of practice to get satisfactory results.

Relatively thick matting really highlights the scherenschnitte, because it creates space between the glass and the background paper. The use of matting will affect your choice of a frame. Make sure that the space in the frame is big enough for the matting, paper, and cardboard backing.

11. The History of Scherenschnitte

A brief overview of the history of scheren-schnitte will allow you to combine practical knowledge with historical information. This chapter will not give the entire history of scherenschnitte and doesn't claim to be complete. Rather, my purpose is to highlight the main trends so you can see the way tradition lives on in contemporary artistic handicraft.

On the one hand, the basic material—paper or parchment—is necessary for the development of scherenschnitte; on the other hand, there could be no scherenschnitte without cutting tools. The first type of scissors, actually a half-round bow with cutting surfaces, is said to have existed in the Second Era of the European Iron Age (the fifth century B.C.). Scissors made of two parts have been known since the time of the Romans. These scissors were developed first of all for medical purposes. The first scissors that were fixed in the middle with a loop appeared in the 14th century.

While parchment has been known for a long time—in the Near East it has been documented since the end of the second millennium before Christ—paper was invented only around A.D. 100 in China. The art of scherenschnitte began relatively early there. Around A.D. 750 paper-making was taken by Chinese war prisoners into the region of Arabic culture and spread toward Europe.

Chinese Scherenschnitte

Paper was being produced in China by the first century after Christ. Therefore, paper cuttings, made partly with shears and partly with knives, were found there very early. Around A. D. 1000, scherenschnitte was very popular, especially in the time of the Sung dynasty (10th-13th century), for which much written documentation exists.

Papercutting was a widespread folk art strongly influenced by painting. Poor people pasted cutout pictures on their lanterns, because painted lanterns were expensive. Paper cuttings called *window flowers* were placed in windows, and paper cuttings on house doors were not only decorative but served as protective images to shield the house from harm. It is fascinating to observe the connection between the motifs in scherenschnitte and the cultural surroundings from which scherenschnitte evolved. We find many motifs in Chinese scherenschnitte taken from Chinese mythology. In our eyes there is a great similarity between Chinese drawings and silhouettes.

Chinese scherenschnitte is cut from very thin paper (silk paper). Approximately six layers are attached together, with the finished scheren-schnitte on top to serve as a pattern. First the outlines and the large inner areas are cut out roughly with scissors. Then the finer work is done. The cutter works most of the inner areas and lines with a small knife.

White, black, and colored papers are used. White paper can be colored after being cut. The little horse at the beginning of the chapter on page 117 was cut from white silk paper and colored afterward. Paper of a different color is often chosen as a background, and frequently gold-colored paper is used to create a luxurious impression. Colorful cuttings, tinted after being cut, are used as a pattern for women to embroider on. In China, parchment is used for cutting out figures that are then assembled into one piece from several parts. They are assembled in such a way that the individual parts can be moved with wooden sticks. The famous shadow theater developed from these stick dolls. The series of movements is sort of an early stage of film. Similar developments took place later in Ceylon and Persia, and around 1900 in Germany as well. Large scherenschnitte were used in China as decoration for sedan chairs, boxes, chests, and saucers that were burned at funerals. The containers held items to be placed in the grave so that the dead person would not lack for anything. In Europe, cut patterns were used to decorate furniture, because they were much more reasonably priced than expensive inlays.

Fig. 11.1 This Chinese dragon is cut from white paper that was colored afterward.

Fig. 11.2 Black scherenschnitte that shows a figure from Chinese mythology.

Scherenschnitte in Europe

How did scherenschnitte come to Europe? According to research that Georg Jacobs carried out at the beginning of the 20th century, scherenschnitte came from China to Austria by way of Indonesia, Persia, and the Balkan Peninsula. From Austria it spread all over Europe. It is difficult to follow the exact path of scherenschnitte since this art turns up at different places and at different times, everywhere with individual traits. The materials and tools for making scherenschnitte art were easy to acquire and accessible to less wealthy people, which may be the main reason that scherenschnitte was a folk art in many places.

White Cutwork

White cutwork is much older than black scherenschnitte. In various parts of Europe early examples are found in the 16th and 17th centuries. This type was made from white paper or parchment, known as *virgin's skin*—that is, parchment made from the skin of unborn calves.

In Germany, R. W. Hus was one of the first well-known artists. He made comical little works of art between 1645 and 1677. White cutwork was especially popular in Holland in the 17th century, where some of the educated classes made it, women who had the leisure for this time-consuming work. Secular themes were used for the most part, often copied from copper engravings. This work was used as gifts or wall decorations and was collected by people of high rank and nobility.

Cutwork is often done in miniature, and these valuable objects began to be made in smaller and smaller sizes, so that they could be placed between glass and silver in a pendant. A magnifying glass is necessary in order to see all the details. These tiny sizes were very much in demand, and several such miniatures have been found in old pocket watches.

However, formats the size of the palm of a hand were more widespread. The outlines were cut with scissors; the inner areas with a fine knife and engraving tool. The cutwork was placed on a colored or black background. Colored cutwork was more rare.

Fig. 11.3 Landscape in original size, Vienna (ca. 1800).

Lace Cutwork

A special type of white cutwork is known as lace cutwork, which was found early in various areas of Europe and especially in convents in the 18th century, where the nuns who were freed of heavy and rough work made these works of art. It is known that handicrafters made lace cutwork for the cloisters.

Fig. 11.4 White cutwork by R. W. Hus (1653).

Lace cutwork was made from white paper or parchment. The parchment was attached with pins or nails to a leather pillow. The holes from the pins can sometimes be seen in the lace cuttings that have been preserved. In addition to scissors, various patterns, punchings, and stampings were used as aids, explaining the total absence of pencil marks on the parchment. Two or more of the same cuttings were often made at the same time, as preserved lace cuttings identical to one another attest. The white cutwork was sometimes placed on a background of black paper and then colored, or cutwork was used to form frames around medallions with a religious motif, which consisted of a drawing, a painted or embroidered miniature, or a copper engraving.

Lace cutwork dates from around 1612. Lace cutwork was inspired largely by pillow lace, silks, and tapestries made in the vicinity of Lyon, France, a center for lace, cloth, and beautiful tapestries at that time. Lace cutwork was widespread, especially in convents in the Alps. These works of art were valuable gifts exchanged for similar creations among the convents. Protestant devotional material or confirmation letters were very rare, so lace cutwork prevailed longer in Catholic regions.

Fig. 11.5 Lace picture from the 18th century, a work from a convent. (Private collection. Photo: Fritz Hobi).

Common people couldn't afford expensive devotional pictures, so they began to make pictures with punches, some of which have been preserved from 1775. They can be recognized by their borders, which are bent downward, and by the frayed edges on the backs.

The History of the Silhouette

From early times, the shadows of loved ones were preserved. We see silhouettes of people in Egyptian graves and on ancient Greek vases. Silhouettes reflect the desire to capture the likeness of people by the use of simple methods. In addition, there is something magical about the shadow of a person. On the one hand, people without shadows are suspected—so people believed in earlier times—of being in alliance with evil. On the other hand, a silhouette can be a special symbol for a tie with a loved one: although it corresponds only to the shadow, there is no shadow without reality.

Proof of the age of this technique is found in Pliny the Elder's history from the year 600 B.C., when he tells of Corintha, who captured the likeness of her departing beloved on a wall. The first silhouettes in Germany were made around 1631. However, the spread of this custom and the beginning of a real fashion dates back only to the early 18th century.

Etienne de Silhouette was minister of finance under Louis XV from March to November 1759. M. de Silhouette was a devotee of outlining shadows, which he learned of during a stay in England. He filled his own little castle with these works of art, some of which he had made himself.

As minister of finance, his task was to replenish the empty state coffers, and he vehemently opposed the wastefulness of his contemporaries. He recommended silhouettes as more reasonable replacements for costly miniatures. In the beginning, his policy for saving met with success, but soon opinion changed. His name became an expression of contempt for these money-saving measures or for penny pinching: there were "culottes a la Silhouette" and a jacket "a la Silhouette," both articles of clothing without pockets or pleats. The inexpensive outlines of people's shadows became known as pictures "a la Silhouette." The career of M. de Silhouette was as short-lived as the will of the monied classes was to save money. But his name was recorded for posterity, not as a concept of saving money to be sure, but as a term for cutting a person's profile: the silhouette.

At this time black paper began to edge out white because, after all, the picture was meant to represent a dark shadow. Earlier, mostly white paper or parchment had been used.

In Germany, cutting portraits became a very popular fashion, a favorite pastime of the middle class. Entire family trees with portraits of the individual family members cut from paper became common at this time. The fashion of making silhouettes spread far and wide but

Fig. 11.6 Silhouette chair.

remained among the upper classes, never becoming a folk art.

Technical aids related to this great interest were developed. In order to make it easier to produce a silhouette, a silhouette chair was used. The person who was to be drawn sat on the chair and was illuminated so that the shadow fell on a glass pane placed between the person and the chair arm. Paper or parchment was attached to the other side of the glass and the shadow could be traced onto that. With the help of a panto-graph the likeness was enlarged to the desired size, then cut out or drawn with black India ink. The cut-out silhouettes have a much livelier effect than those that have simply been drawn.

At that time, as now, the easiest method of drawing a silhouette was to project it onto the wall and transfer this onto paper. If you want to make silhouettes yourself, this is the best way to begin and to practice.

Later, silhouettes were filled in with India ink. For example, the hair would be drawn in. During the first half of the 19th century, the sil-houette was developed further by the addition of color. The background was filled in with sev-eral colors, for example, or colorful clothing was pasted on, so that only the head was black. The figures were decorated with lace or laurel leaves.

Around 1840 Sophie Gehret founded a silhou-ette school in Biel, which was attended mostly by women, since the fine, decorative scissors work seemed especially suitable for them. In the course of time, silhouettes developed into genre pictures, that is, entire figures and groups of fig-ures, whose borders were frequently framed by roots and branches.

The Swiss Johann Caspar Lavater (1741-1801), founder of the study of physiognomy, had a spe-cial relationship to silhouettes. He became famous for his "Physiognomical Fragments," in which he did broad research trying to ascertain the character of persons from their facial attrib-utes. A silhouette was practically ideal for Lavater because it simplified the observation of facial characteristics for analysis and allowed concentration on the essentials.

Fig. 11.7 Silhouette studies by Johann Caspar Lavater.

Scherenschnitte in Germany

The earliest scherenschnitte in Germany is by an artist known simply as "Hus." Only in this century was it determined that his complete name was Rudolf Wilhelm Herr von Stubenberg (1645-1677). R. W. Hus made decorative white cutwork from paper and parchment and demonstrated great skill in making ornaments and themes with figures.

In the 17th and 18th centuries there was much anonymous cutwork of the folk art type. But for other works we do know the names of the artists.

A very important artist was Luise Duttenhofer (1776-1829). She made many silhouettes but enriched them by using a special background:

by placing the figures on a mosaic floor drawn in perspective, she succeeded in creating depth, which actually went against the nature of scherenschnitte. Typical of the work of Luise Duttenhofer are the social-critical themes, showing elements of caricature, and this is one aspect of her work that sets it apart from the dominant type of silhouettes.

The Romantic painter and writer Otto Runge (1777-1810) considered the scissors as an extension of his fingers and cut complicated landscapes. He especially loved plants, which he reproduced very realistically with roots, stems, blossoms, and seeds, often cut from white paper and pasted onto black paper. Other important scherenschnitte artists were Karl Fröhlich (1821-1898) and Wilhelm Müller (1804-1865).

Fig. 11.8 R. W. Hus, Allegorical Representation (1653).

Fig. 11.9 Luise Duttenhofer, "Goethe in Stuttgart" (1797).

Fig. 11.10 Luise Duttenhofer, "Gaupp".

Fig. 11.11 Phillip Otto Runge, Leafy Shrub with Orange Lily.

Fig. 11.12 Karl Frühlich.

Fig. 11.13 Wilhelm Müller.

Fig. 11.14 Paul Konewka, "Faust and Gretchen" (1861).

Fröhlich was a picture carver, an illustrator, and a writer. The shoemaker Wilhelm Mäller, who made very beautiful scherenschnitte, sold his works for very little money during the evenings in inns, to be able to purchase medicine for his dangerously ill son. Unfortunately, the son died very soon in spite of the efforts of his father.

Paul Konewka (1841-1871) made a name for himself as illustrator of many poetic master-works such as "Faust," "Falstaff," and "A Midsummer Night's Dream."

Scherenschnitte in Poland

In Poland, scherenschnitte reached its high point between the end of the first half of the last century and the beginning of World War I. For a long period of time, nobody paid much attention to this skill, and as a folk art it lived in the shadow of other art. Only at the beginning of this century was Polish scherenschnitte given much attention outside the peasant population.

We do not know where Polish scherenschnitte began. Especially before Easter and Christmas, when homes in the country were spruced up and whitewashed, women, both old and young, who did not have their own households and little children to look after, made scherenschnitte. They inspired each other so that in the course of time the level of the Polish school was raised. Ornaments, borders, and colorful pieces for collages were made with sheep shearing shears. (Even today most Polish scherenschnitte is still made with rough sheep shears.) These were put on the painted walls of rooms and houses. Six months later when new cutwork was created, the old was removed and often used to decorate the stalls. In Poland, scherenschnitte was made only as wall decoration for houses. Today, now that houses are built in another style, the traditional scherenschnitte has disappeared from the walls.

Polish scherenschnitte was mostly in the shape of a square or a wheel, and frequent motifs are roosters and hens or a wedding couple. Abstract ornaments were multiplied in the form of endless borders, which repeated the motifs numerous times. In the borders, many little men and women appear too, the same motifs that appeared in this form in Western Europe. Collage-type cuttings are widespread and very well developed, as described in the chapter "Colored Scherenschnitte." The basic motifs in black are artfully decorated by pasting many colorful areas over them (Fig. 11.15). In Poland, individual pieces of the colorful, cut paper were available, and you could put them together anyway you liked. Eggs are decorated with scherenschnitte in Poland.

131

Fig. 11.15 Black Polish scherenschnitte with colorful inlays decorated in collage style.

Scherenschnitte in Switzerland

The cradle of Swiss folk scherenschnitte was Saanenland and Pay d'Enhaut around 1800. It is interesting that this folk art was first made mostly by simple men who displayed fascinating mastery, yet as a rule never got rich from it. Silhouette cutting, whose history appears on page 124, can be found very early in Switzerland. However, it was practiced mainly among the upper classes.

The blacksmith Johann Jakob Hauswirth (1809-1871), from Saanen, is described as a gigantic man with massive hands that did not fit into any scissors, so he attached wire rings to the scissors to accommodate his large fingers. In spite of the hard work he did, his motor skills were so developed that he created wonderfully delicate works, which he often used to pay for a place to sleep and a meal. Most of his work uses the folding and cutting technique. During his itinerant lifetime in Saanenland he left behind a trail of scherenschnitte that show motifs from his surroundings: alpine inclines, peasant life, and animals and people from this environment. In his old age he often transformed colored paper into cutwork. His works were often kept in Bibles or framed, because there were no other suitable places to keep them. Hauswirth's scherenschnitte are very valuable today, but he himself died poor.

In 1871, the year Hauswirth died, Louis Saugy (1871-1953) was born in Saanenland. As a young person he probably became familiar with the widely known scherenschnitte of Hauswirth. Saugy was strongly inspired by these works and motifs. He, too, led sort of a wandering life, if a bit more comfortable, because he was a postman. Saugy became a story teller through his scherenschnitte; he tied together plot and decoration. Because of hearing difficulties, he retired at age 57. He was not unhappy about this because he was able to do more cutwork. In contrast to Hauswirth, he became very famous in his lifetime, and his works sold very well even though the prices rose. After his wife died, he had a housekeeper who cut animals from several layers of paper that he then refined and arranged into collages. Every detail was equally important to him.

A further representative of folk scherenschnitte from Saanenland was the carpenter Christian Schwizgebel (1914-1993). His grandfather, who was a teacher, encouraged him and had him draw all kinds of animals. In school, he found teachers who recognized his talent and supported it. He spent ten summers in a mountain pasture, where he trained his powers of observation and studied the behavior of animals. His ability to observe can be seen clearly in his cutwork of animals that express the mood of the environment as well. Smaller works were made without

Fig. 11.16 Johann Jakob Hauswirth (1856).

sketches; he worked many days on the composition of larger works. He always used the same theme with variations, as artists using certain motifs often do. His ornamental cuttings became true masterpieces.

In addition to many men who carried on this folk art, there were women who made a name for themselves as scherenschnitte artists. The female handicraft artist from Basel, Julia Feiner-Wiederkehr (1901-1991), learned about scherenschnitte during the first World War, when she visited an exhibition about Johann Jakob Hauswirth and became very enthusiastic about this art form. In her scherenschnitte she expresses the need to broaden this folk art. She tells of her daily life and uses fairy tales and biblical themes.

Fig. 11.17 Louis Saugy (1951).

Fig. 11.18 Christian Schwizgebel (1957).

Fig. 11.19 Julia Feiner-Wiederkehr.

Annelore Fässler (1915-1990), from Basel, was an independent craftswoman who in 1930 mounted her scherenschnitte on cloth. At the age of 11 she won first prize in a scherenschnitte contest. Her cuttings reflected joy and sorrow and used very timely themes such as the dying forests. She was one of those rare artists who could cut silhouettes freehand without making a sketch first. These folk artists laid the foundation and are still models for many people today. Contemporary artists deal with tradition and continue it but also give this folk art new life by further developing motifs. The Scherenschnitte Society promotes a new blossoming of this art by regularly organizing Swiss exhibitions.

Fig. 11.20 Annelore Fässler-Oehler.

Jewish Scherenschnitte

Jewish scherenschnitte, like the Jewish people, has spread over the entire world and developed according to individual traditions in various places.

The 17th century generated paper cuttings in southern Europe influenced by Jewish life in the diaspora. In Northern Italy, texts from the Book of Esther were used; they were encircled by ornaments, vines, and animal representations. Similar work could be found in marriage contracts of well-to-do families.

Since the 19th century, a distinctive type of liturgical scherenschnitte has evolved in Poland and Russia. Misrach leaves, which pointed in the direction of Jerusalem, were especially popular in prayer rooms. Scherenschnitte was used to mark important events in one's life.

A popular use for scherenschnitte was as amulets for women in childbirth to ward off harm for newborns. Oaths were written on the decorative papers which were framed by scherenschnitte. This valuable amulet, called a "kimpetbriefel" (child-bed letter), was hung above the bed of a woman in childbirth.

On the weekly feast of the Sabbath, motifs such as the Star of David and the menorah were cut and hung in the windows. Most of this valuable cutwork was lost with the extermination of the Jews in eastern Europe. The tradition was renewed in Israel and the United States, where Eastern and Islamic ornamental influences can be clearly recognized.

Fig. 11.21 Jewish scherenschnitte: Shiviti from Poland (18th Century).

Index of Illustrations

If not otherwise noted, all scherenschnitte are by the author.

Fig. 7.1, 7.2, 11.3, 11.4, 11.8, 11.13 and 11.14. from:
Martin Knapp (ed.) *Deutsche Schatten-und Scherenbilder.* Dachau/Munich: Der Gelbe Verlag.

Fig. 11.6 and 11.11 from:
Schoeller, Wilfried F. (Ed.). Das *Silhouettenkabinett.* Frankfurt/Main: Insel Verlag, 1985.

Fig. 11.7 and 11.12 from:
Hopf, Angela and Andreas. *Schattenbilder.* Munich: Bruckmann, 1986.

Fig. 11.9 and 11.10 from:
Collected documents of Luise Duttenhofer. With kind permission of the Schiller National Museum, Marbach am Neckar.

Fig. 11.16, 11.17 and 11.18 from:
Rubi, Christian. *Scherenschnitte aus hundert Jahren.* Bern: Verlag Hans Huber, 1959.

Fig. 11.19 and 11.20 from:
Gewerbemuseum [Craft Museum] Winterthur (Publishers), Catalog of the first Swiss Scherenschnitte Exhibition, Winterthur, 1985.

Fig. 11.21 from:
Haifa Museum of Music and Ethnology (Publishers). *World Papercuts.* Haifa: 1986.